The 7 Essential Steps to Get More Clients

For Coaches & Consultants

By Jeannette Koczela

*Founder/President,
International Association of Professional Life Coaches®*

Copyright © 2016 Jeannette Koczela

Printed in the United States of America. Published by Jeannette Koczela and Global Management Inc. All rights reserved. No portion of this book may be reproduced mechanically, electronically, or by any other means, including photocopying, without written permission of the publisher. It is illegal to copy this book, post it to a website, or distribute it by any other means without permission from the publisher.

Limits of Liability and Disclaimer of Warranty
> The author and publisher shall not be liable for any misuse of this material. This book is strictly for informational and educational purposes.

Warning – Disclaimer
> The purpose of this book is to educate and entertain. The author and/or publisher do not guarantee that anyone following these techniques, suggestions, tips, ideas, or strategies will become successful. The author and/or publisher shall have neither liability nor responsibility to anyone with respect to any loss or damage caused, or alleged to be caused, directly or indirectly by the information contained in this book.

Cover design by Jeannette Koczela

ISBN-13: 978-1539523413

Table of Contents

Chapter 1: How Do I Get More Clients?............7

Chapter 2: How Do I Define My Target Market and Niche?............10

Chapter 3: How Can I Get More Traffic to My Site?............19

Chapter 4: Where Do I Find High-Quality Leads?............25

Chapter 5: How Can I Build My List?............35

Chapter 6: How Can I Use Social Media to Get Clients?............51

Chapter 7: How Do I Convert Leads Into Clients?............59

Chapter 8: How Can I Retain Clients?............67

Chapter 9: What's the Next Step?............74

About the Author

Jeannette Koczela spent several decades as an Impressionist oil painter and working as a free-lance artist. Then an interest in computers led her to become a graphic and web designer, and to create online products including a flash card set, and a home study course, which included some life coaching based on Law of Attraction principles.

Intrigued by the new field of life coaching, she took a certified spiritual life coach training that inspired her first published book, "Money Mindset Makeover." While coaching life coaches, she began to see a need for more ways for them to connect with potential clients and to learn more business skills.

Her second book, "Life Coach Business Blueprint" combined all the business and marketing skills she learned while running her own coaching business, and teaches new coaches how to run and market a coaching business.

The idea of founding an association culminated in creating her "International Association of Professional Life Coaches®." The association offers an online directory, monthly business and marketing trainings, opportunities for publishing and speaking, and other resources for life coaches. Become a member at: www.iaplifecoaches.org

Personal website: www.jeannettekoczela.com
Email: jeannettekoczela@iaplifecoaches.org

Chapter 1
How Do I Get More Clients?

When I ask coaches or consultants what their biggest marketing challenge is, they almost always say, "How do I get more clients?" What they really want to know is, "How can I do what I love, help a lot of people make life-changing transformations, and have a profitable, successful business? And what do I need to know to do this?"

As a coach, I went through the same growing pains most new coaches went through to create a profitable business and now I'm in a position to share my knowledge and expertise with you.

Here's how I learned (the hard way) how to get more clients:

In my forties, I had to end a 17-year marriage and move halfway across the country from big-city life as a free-lance artist to a small town. Back in the city, I had my own business drawing house portraits for expensive homes in expensive neighborhoods. But when I moved to Iowa, there were not enough concentrated neighborhoods for my art business, so I ended up getting a job.

While I had that job, I became fascinated with computer graphics, and took a two-year program to learn graphic and web design. Then, in my "new life" in Iowa, I started my own business as a graphic and web designer.

But very soon I ran into the same problem of not having enough possible clients in my small town. So, I got a brilliant idea: "I'll create my own product and sell it online." I had heard stories of many people who were making money, selling things online. How hard could it be?

I had it all figured out. I took quotes from a public domain book, Wallace Wattles', "The Science of Getting Rich," and, using my own photographs, I manufactured a card set with quotes and graphics on each card. Thinking it would be a great-selling product, I ordered 1000 sets of them. My plan for selling was to approach a woman who had a website with a big list of people who liked the Wattles book. She was selling her audio version of the book, and it was very popular.

When the cards were ready, I sent her an email with my proposal that she sell my card sets on her site and receive a generous commission. No response. I sent it again. No response. Finally I found her phone number and called her, and her secretary said that she wasn't interested.

What!! I just went into debt to make this cool product, and now I have no idea how to sell it! I was in shock.

Now let's stop for a moment and analyze what happened. The point I'd like to make is that I didn't do my homework---I didn't do the **market research**. I had no evidence that people would want to buy my product, and I had no idea how to market it other than rely on someone else to do it.

Not a good plan---and **no** plan B. So that's why you need to do your "homework" first, before you even think about how to promote your business.

So, how do you get more clients? The answer is that you don't do what I did. Before you try to sell something—whether products or services—you must first do your due-diligent **market research**. And that's the first step in the 7 essential steps you need to take to get more clients.

The steps in this book are about the prep-work you must do before you start selling. The next seven chapter titles are questions that often come up about marketing. The answers to these questions all happen to be the steps you should take to get more clients. So after reading this book, you will know exactly what to do to successfully promote and market your product or service.

Now let's answer the seven questions.

Chapter 2
How Do I Define My Target Market and Niche?

In the course of my coaching I have discovered that the majority of coaches who have trouble getting more clients, have not narrowed their target market or niche enough to be able to make their marketing effective. To market effectively, you must focus on what problem you solve (niche) and who you want to work with (target).

There could be many people who have the problem that you solve, and it's much easier to find those people if you first carefully define who they are. And, if they can see exactly how you can help them, they will respond to your efforts. That's what target and niche are all about.

One of my first clients was having trouble deciding on her target and niche. I worked with her for almost 6 months while she went back and forth between two areas of expertise.

So much time was wasted because she couldn't make up her mind. And she was resisting the concept of focusing on one target with one specialty that she could offer. She was afraid of turning away potential clients if she zeroed in on only one group for her target.

Maybe you are someone who has resisted this, perhaps for fear of losing possible clients due to over specializing. It could even be a form of procrastination or self-sabotage. Whatever the root cause is, it's something that you must take a closer look at if you want to get more clients.

Let's see if we can push through any resistance that you might have, so you can get on to the marketing of your business.

In the coaching industry, the word "niche" is sometimes used when "target" is what is meant. So, what's the difference between a target market and a niche? Look at it this way: your *niche* is the service you specialize in offering to your *target market*.

Your niche is the problem you solve or what you're an expert at. That expertise is determined by your experience and your interest. You may have a background in a certain field.

For example, say you had a job working with people in recovery situations. Perhaps you developed a system that accelerated their recovery progress, and now you want to coach people recovering from trauma. Your skill for accelerating recovery will be your niche; people recovering from trauma are your target market. You can research and decide on the target market and niche simultaneously, but let's start by discussing your niche.

Define Your Niche/Expertise

For many solopreneurs, there are several challenges associated with defining your niche. One of them is the above mentioned fear of eliminating potential clients, and thus limiting your possibilities. Another one is the fear of picking the wrong niche. Despite these fears, I am recommending that you not only choose a niche but also make it a narrow one.

Why a narrow niche?
1- Attract ideal clients
The first reason to narrow your niche or choose a specialty is to attract specific (ideal) clients, ones that you can serve best and thereby attract more of the same. You see, a wide niche, may actually attract **fewer** potential clients, because you aren't addressing a particular urgent need. Many people need medicine, but they will respond only to marketing that addresses their specific ailment.

Imagine going to a drugstore with a headache and going to the pain reliever aisle. Given the choice, you will most likely buy a product labeled as "relieving a headache". You would be much less likely to buy a product that just says, "Pain Relief". People want products that offer a specific solution to fix a specific problem.

A narrow niche also serves as a welcome gateway. By offering a specific group a specific solution to an urgent problem, you're simply helping them walk through a gateway, and then inside that gateway you can show them all the different other ways you can help them.

Inside the gate are all the great breakthroughs and transformations your clients need to make. That's where it all happens.

But if you don't convey what your niche is clearly enough, they can't see that the gateway is for them in the first place, and they'll never even consider walking through it. You need to get them through the gate first.

2- Be seen as the expert

The second reason to narrow your niche is that when you solve a specific problem of a specific group of people, you have a better chance of being seen as the expert. And experts can attract more clients and can charge more for their services than generalists. As true in the medical profession a General Practitioner does not make as much money as a Neurosurgeon. Why? The perceived value is greater because it's assumed that specialists have more advanced training, and more experience in a particular field.

So when you narrow your niche, you increase your chances of being perceived as the expert, and consequently you will attract more clients and be able to charge more.

Another thing to consider when determining your niche is your uniqueness in your marketplace. What do you want to be known for or be the expert in? For example, in my association, the competitive edge was in being the only association for life coaches that combined a directory, a professional organization, group activities for more visibility, and a business skills training and support system.

Two methods for determining your niche
A. Answer questions

The first method is to answer the following questions. The answers can help you choose a niche:
1) What do you consider yourself to be an expert at?
2) What have you had the most experience with?
3) What's the biggest struggle or painful problem you've had to overcome personally?
4) If you were told to write a "how-to" book in a week, what subject would you choose?

5) What are some of your past jobs/careers?
6) What obstacles have you successfully overcome in life, and how did you do it?
7) Which of your life experiences could others learn from?

Then once you have these answers, determine a common theme. Once you have a theme or topic, you can brainstorm what area of that topic, you can focus in on more.

Let's say you found that the theme that came coming up for you was relationships. You know you are good at helping people with their relationships. So then you might narrow it down to dealing with divorce. Then you can narrow down again to focus on single ladies in a certain age group that have recently gone through a divorce. You can see that this is how to narrow the focus.

B. Drill categories
You can also narrow your niche by drilling down categories. You start by determining the overall category that your work is in. The four areas listed below, according to statistics, are the ones where you will find the most people spending money on solving problems.

- Health & Fitness
- Relationships
- Money & Business
- Transformation

Next, you start narrowing down possible niches into subcategories until you come to one that is most specific but still has enough people in it to make it profitable.

Examples:
1. Health & Fitness → Losing weight → Losing weight after a pregnancy

2. Relationships → Parenting → Parenting teens → Parenting teens with a drinking problem
3. Money& Business → Marketing → Online Marketing → Social Media Marketing → getting clients through LinkedIn ads
4. Transformation → Money Mindset issues → Removing money blocks with mindset tools

Once you have decided on a niche, you can define your target market.

Define Your Ideal Client/Target Market
Defining your target market is simply locating the people who are most likely to need your service. You can separate people by age, income, profession, location or other demographics, as well as psychographics (mindsets).

Why a narrow target?
1 – Easier Marketing
It's easier to market to a well-defined target, because then you can find them in groups. Finding groups of leads is a better use of your time than going after them one by one. Once you've clearly defined who your solution is for, it's also easier for them to find you.

Also, if you can zero in on one problem and one solution for a specific group of people, it's easier to create marketing materials. You can speak their language and attract them, rather than chase after them. They feel that you are speaking directly to them, and that makes it easier for them to raise their hand and say, "Yes I need your help."

2- Better clients
When you know who your target market (or ideal clients) are, you don't spend time pursuing those who aren't ideal

clients. You stop trying to attract just any client and start attracting clients who are a beautiful vibrational match for you and your business. You enjoy working with each other, and the relationship is mutually beneficial. Then the conversation flows, it's easy to be with them, and, at the energetic level, it's more like talking to a friend.

Here are some ways to zero in on your target market:

Create an "avatar"
A great way to define your ideal client is to create a profile or "avatar" to go beyond demographics, such as gender, income, location, age, by listing the qualities that you would want them to have. Consider qualities such as reliability, sincerity, honesty, willingness to change, flexibility, and sense of humor.

You can also chunk it down by breaking the possible target market into smaller segments. Do this by identifying a group of people with 1) very specific identifying characteristics, such as people starting a home business, people with dog problems, or people who need to lose weight; or 2) problems that you can solve, such as people recovering from breast cancer, people deciding on a new career, or people in search of their life purpose.

A version of you
Another thing to consider when defining your ideal client is that they are probably a version of you…some form of you in the past, who was facing the same problem that you now can solve.

For example, maybe you've gone through a painful experience in a relationship, and now you coach others how to avoid that experience. Or you may have taken years to find your life purpose, and now you coach people to find it in a few weeks. Or you learned the "hard" way how to present teleseminars and now you can coach people how to do it the "easy" way.

One of the biggest mistakes solopreneurs make is they often overlook their life experiences as part of their expertise. They ask, "Why would anyone care about what I've done, or what I've accomplished?" But the truth is, people reach out and follow a coach because they resonate with their story. People want to learn from people who solved a problem similar to the one they have.

As you get to know that ideal client you can language your offers specifically to them. The more you know about your ideal client, the easier it will be to attract them to you.

Your Defining Statement

Now you can use what you've learned from defining your niche and target market to create a statement that tells people what you do in a specific and compelling way. Fill in this sentence:

I help _____(your target market) who are struggling with _____(problem you solve or niche) so they can _____(results they will receive from working with you).

For example: I help <u>life coaches</u> who are struggling with <u>starting up their business on a small budget</u> so they can <u>attract clients easily and quickly</u>.

Summary
Step 1: Define your target and niche
So, the first step in getting more clients is to clearly and specifically define your niche---what your specialty is---and your target---who you want to market to.

Chapter 3
How Can I Get More Traffic to My Site?

Having been a web-designer for several years, I thought that once I set up my website, it would be easy to get traffic and leads to my site. I was happy to be saving money by creating my own site, and cheerfully forged ahead with making one. And again when I set up my coaching practice, I designed my own site. But getting traffic to either site was a monumental task. I needed a marketing strategy.

I joined services like ones where you had to visit so many other people's sites in order to get enough credits for people to visit your site, and that was way more time-consuming than it was worth.

Then I took a course in SEO, but by the time I was done with it, the rules and algorithms of the browsers had changed---and they kept changing, so often that it was hard to keep up with them. It took me several years to discover what was needed.

Now when coaches ask me "How can I get more traffic to my site?" my answer is, "Do you really want JUST traffic?" There are many ways to get traffic to your site.

But what you really want is not just traffic but HIGH-QUALITY LEADS that can be turned into buyers. That's why you need to do market research. Only after you have laid that foundation, should you begin to use strategies that will get traffic to your site.

Note: And just so you know, if you were still having trouble deciding on your target and niche in the last chapter, sometimes it helps to do your market research first and then make those decisions. So these two chapters may have to be done simultaneously. Just go with what makes the most sense to you personally.

The Market Research you need to do

Before you start setting up a website and software for your business, you will first need to do some research which will help you in choosing a URL, keywords for SEO (search engine optimization), and language for your sales materials.

Keywords

Your keywords or keyword phrases will help get traffic to your site, attract the right clients who can use your services, and help you language your offerings.

A keyword is one or two words like "marketing", "empty-nesters", or "life coach". A keyword phrase is just a longer version such as "recovering from trauma", "gluten-free diets for baby-boomers", or "small business marketing solutions". You choose them based on what your business does.

Here are some questions to answer that can help you find keywords/phrases that are relevant to your business:

1) What words or phrases do you want to be found under?
2) What issue does your life coaching address?
3) What problem do you solve?
4) What kind of coaching do you do? Relationship? Health? Business? Executive? Career? Spiritual? Law of Attraction?
5) Who do you want to coach? Empty-nesters? Teens? Accountants?
6) What are the benefits of your approach and your programs?
7) What results can people expect when working with you?

Many people choose their keywords based solely on the answer to question one. But the answers to all these questions together are going to give you a better idea of how to choose the keywords/phrases to use in your marketing.

Google has a keyword research tool, called Keyword Planner, through its "Ad Words" program (you need to have an AdWords account to use the tool, but you don't need to be actively paying for ads). You can use it to find out what keywords people are using to search for the services you provide. Statistics to make note of are: the number of searches for each keyword or phrase, and the number of competitors.

Ideally you want keywords that have a high number of searches and a low number of competitors. You may want to select keywords that are more out of the ordinary so it will be easier to rank high in them. For example, instead of using "small business" as a keyword phrase, I chose to use "small business marketing solutions" because it had a high number of searches but a low number of competitors.

Other places to research include forums or LinkedIn groups in your field, where you can see what questions people are asking and how they are worded, and Amazon.com, where you can see what books in your field are best sellers. You may also want to visit sites of your competitors to see how they language their services and what keywords and phrases they use.

Tip: I put all of my keywords in an Excel spreadsheet and compared the number of monthly searches, number of competitors for that keyword, etc. That gave me a framework for choosing keywords that would give my site a good ranking. General keywords such as "life coach" will be hard to rank very high in because of the heavy competition. But a narrower keyword such as, "relationship coach" or "career transitions" will rank better.

Once you decide on 5 to 10 keywords you want to use, keep them handy for the marketing strategies that we will discuss later in this book.

Best methods for free traffic
SEO (search engine optimization)
Now that you've done your keyword research, you can use your selected keywords on your website to optimize your site ranking. Using keywords on your website is what will give you "organic" (that means free) traffic. It's the best kind of traffic, because these visitors actually searched for your keywords. This means they are looking for someone like you to help them, and they may be ready to buy a possible solution to their problem.

But it's important to use keywords strategically and sparingly. Search engines will not give you a good ranking if you use your keywords too often on your pages. The purpose of keywords is to aid the search engines in directing people to your site who are looking for what you are offering. Your copy should sound authentic and be clear on what you do, who you serve, and how you can help.

Blogging
Blogging is one of the best ways to boost your site's search engine ranking, without having to pay money. Search engines want to see regular, updated material on your site. And the easiest way to get new information on your site is by blogging. When you write a blog, you will want to use keywords that you found in your initial market research. They can go in the title as well as the text. Then, since every blog post has its own individual keywords, it's an additional way to improve your search engine ranking.

Guest Blogging
This is where you write a blog post for someone else's blog. You can have an "about the author" section at the end with the URL to your site and/or your free offer. If the readers liked your post, they will come to your site to check you out. Of course you only want to post on sites that have your target market as part of their readership.

Posting in online groups
Post a notice about your opt-in gift in various online groups, such as those on LinkedIn and Facebook. Look for groups that are on your topic or have your target market in them.

Best methods for paid traffic
Facebook and LinkedIn ads are two of the best methods for paid traffic because both venues offer ways to target very specific markets. You can pretty much select all the criteria that you are looking for in your ideal clients and Facebook and LinkedIn will show your ad only to those people who meet your criteria. For example, if you are a relationship coach, and your target is professional women in their 40's who have recently gone through a divorce in your local area,

you can select professional women between 40 and 50 who have recently become single and live in (your location).

With both venues you can select a daily limit as to how much you spend. LinkedIn ads are more expensive. However, one of my coaches who tested both venues found that he got a higher return on investment from the LinkedIn ads, i.e. the LinkedIn ads got better leads that turned into higher-priced sales than with Facebook ads.

If you are just starting out and/or are on a budget, you may want to start out with Facebook ads. But advertising is tricky, and unless you know what you're doing you can lose money with it, so find an expert, or someone with plenty of experience to help you.

Other methods that are available, but not generally as effective, are Google Adwords, Google Adsense, and pay-per-click advertising. You can find out more about them online.

Summary
Step 2: Do your market research to get targeted traffic.
This is the step that most coaches and consultants skip over and also why so many of them fail to get traffic to their site. If you build it, they won't necessarily come, unless they know why they should. Your market research insures that you will design and set up your site in in a way that gets appropriate traffic.

Chapter 4
Where Do I Find High-Quality Leads?

In the last chapter, I said that in order to find clients that are aligned with you, your message and your work, you need to find not just traffic but **high quality** leads. What is a high-quality lead? A high-quality lead is someone who is looking for a solution to the problem that you solve and would most benefit from your particular solution. It's someone in your target market that is ready to take the next step, such as subscribing to your list, finding out more, and making a purchase.

Let's face it---there are probably many others solving the same problem that you solve. But you are solving it in your own unique way and it's going to be the best solution for a certain group of people, the ones you were meant to serve.

In order to find these people you need to look in the right places. So the real problem is where do you find high quality leads that are looking for your solution and that you can meet, build a relationship with, and turn into a client? This chapter will tell you where to find these leads both online and offline.

My coach training program was 9 months in duration. During that time, I learned a lot about helping people make transformations in their lives. I did not learn much about marketing. What I did learn was that the fastest way to get clients and jumpstart your business was to get them offline.

That's because offline you are connecting with people in person, and that has the most lasting effect and impression. It's easier to establish the "know, like, and trust factor" when you are interacting with people in person. And they are naturally more likely to become higher quality leads. Here are 3 of the best strategies for securing high-quality leads offline.

Where Offline?
Networking Meetings

The fastest way to get more clients---whether you're just starting out, or have been in business for years---is through live networking. Since you've identified your target market, now you can go to their hangouts and meet them. There are probably networking opportunities where you live that you can attend to see if your target market is there.

Large metropolitan areas may have several different kinds of networking meetings that you can attend, and it's best to check them all out to see which ones contain people in your target.

But that's just half of it. You also want to go to places where there are people who can refer clients to you. That's where entrepreneurs often make a big mistake in networking. They approach people who they think are their target market, try to sell them on their services, and if there is no interest, they move on.

Here's a better approach: When you meet people at a networking event, ask them if they know anyone who could use your services. That way you let them off the hook from you trying to sell them something, and it becomes a conversation of peers, rather than salesperson and potential client. If they're interested in your services for themselves, they'll tell you. Effective networking not only targets potential clients, but also peers, colleagues, and other professionals with whom you can share resources, knowledge, information, and referrals.

Networking is an opportunity to find people who are in sync with you. It's about building relationships, not just getting sales. The old paradigm of the scarcity mentality was, "How can I get their attention? What can I say to impress them? How can I get what I want?"

The new paradigm comes from an abundance mentality, which asks, "What do I have to offer? How can I help others be successful? How can I be my authentic self and still provide value? What does this person want and need? How did their situation arise? How can I solve their problem?"

Ideally, in networking situations, you will be doing most of the listening instead of most of the talking. Instead of telling people what you do, ask them questions about themselves. Be interested in them, find out as much as you can about them. You want them to feel energized and supported after a conversation with you. By having this kind of interaction, you will be able to tell if your services are a good fit for them.

If they're not a good fit for you, you may refer them to someone else who is. Networking from that perspective becomes more than just seeking clients. Now you are networking for others with a mindset of no expectations in return, and they will be doing the same for you as the reciprocity principle kicks in. In this way you are building your very own network.

There are many networking clubs nationally and internationally. For example, **Business Network International (BNI)** (www.BNI.com) has chapters all over the world. You join a group that has one person from each profession, so for example, in a particular group, you would be the only life coach. During the meetings everyone tells what they do and speaks about the services they offer, and then everyone shares referrals. BNI charges $500 a year for this service.

Meet-up (www.meetup.com) chapters are similar to BNI but with different guidelines and fees. You can start your own Meet-up group and it can be on any theme.

Another resource is the worldwide coaches organization, **International Coaching Federation (ICF)** (www.coachfederation.org). They have chapters in all major cities. If you are an ICF member, their meetings are a place to build a referral network.

You can Google any of the above organizations to find a chapter in your area.

The next step is to identify places to do your own networking. This may take some research on your part. You can also start your own networking group if your area doesn't have one. One of our association members started a local networking group that grew to 500 members, and they applied and became an official Meet-up group.

Make a list of relevant groups, organizations, meetings, and events that you know about whose attendees are your target market or your colleagues.

Here are some ideas:
- Live events
- BNI groups
- Meet-up groups
- ICF chapters
- Your local Chamber of Commerce
- Friends of your local library
- Local business showcases
- Entrepreneur clubs
- Rotary Clubs
- Toastmasters
- Serving on local committees
- Create your own support group on your topic
- Support groups that have your ideal clients
- Any social gathering, even birthday parties

Even in a small town there may be networking opportunities such as having a booth at a local event, festival, local business exhibitions, or eco-fests.

Referrals

One of the best ways to spread the word about your business is word of mouth. Now, to most new solopreneurs, that sounds like something that you have absolutely no control over and, technically, that's true. But there's also a way to systematically spread your message via word of mouth and it's called referral marketing.

Start by making a list of people who you think could become your advocates, i.e. clients, past clients, associates, colleagues, acquaintances, etc. Try for a list of 100.

Then start connecting with the people on your list and let them know what you do and how to refer people to you.

Here are some ways to do that:
- Arrange meetings with colleagues
- Seek JV partners with the same target market
- Stay in touch with former clients
- Give referrals
- Share valuable information and resources

Connecting with people you know is the way to start, but eventually you'll be meeting possible referral partners from people you don't know. You can then build a relationship with them and teach them how to refer you to people they know.

Live Events

Going to live events where your coaches or mentors are giving talks, seminars, courses, or workshops are great places to meet other like-minded individuals who might be potential clients.

I try to go to one live event each year, and I have always found enough leads who were also attending the event that became clients of mine. The income from those clients more than paid for the investment in traveling and attending the live event.

One way to find events is to get on the mailing lists of the influencers in your industry. Pick ones who have an agenda that will also be beneficial and interesting to you. You can also Google event calendars for events in your area or other locations.

Where Online?

My efforts at offline networking did not go so well when I first started out. There were already 10 other life coaches in our town (pop. 10,000) whom I knew and had to compete with. And I hate to compete with friends. So, I focused my efforts online. Here are some of the best places to find your target market online that I have found.

Online Groups

We talked before about defining your target market and doing that very narrowly so that you can find groups of these people. The two best places for groups are on Facebook and LinkedIn. What your topic is and where your potential clients are hanging out, will determine which of those two would be better for your marketing efforts.

Also, you may already be a member of groups on Facebook and LinkedIn and such groups are places to tap into. Get involved and see which members are potential clients.

Select a few of those groups to establish a presence in and start connecting with people. Share valuable content, information, and resources to begin building a relationship with them.

You can also eventually form your own group and that's really the ultimate goal because then you have your own group of people who are like your tribe or your fans. These are the people that are really interested in what you have to offer, and that's because you've already shared plenty of valuable content and resources with them.

Forums

Another place to find leads online is in forums. If you are connected with any forums of classes you are taking or have taken, that's another place where you're going to find leads. In forums you usually have people who are like-minded or who have a common interest. And so those are people that you can also connect with and see if they need your help.

Guest Blogs

The third place to find leads online is through guest blogging. If you can be a guest blogger on a site that has an appeal to your target market you will probably get some interest from the readers of that blog. You always want to make an offer for one of your freebies at the end of your guest blog post so that people have an enticement to come over to your website and see what more you have to offer them.

Podcasts/Radio Shows

Another way to find leads online is to be a guest for someone's podcast or radio show. There are plenty of people who have their own podcasts or radio shows and they're always looking for guests to interview that have valuable knowledge, expertise, and information that would appeal to their audience. You can do a search on the Internet for podcasts and radio shows with your topic. Getting interviewed by someone who already has a following is a great way to find leads online.

JV Partnerships

Joint venturing is really one of the best ways to expand your reach. You can find joint venture partners and ask if you could give a presentation or webinar to their audience. Just make sure that they have a list that includes your target market.

If you have a signature talk you can turn it into a webinar and give presentations as often as you can find people who will let you present to their audience.

Even if you're just starting out, you can begin to cultivate joint venture partnerships. You will want to find partners that have similar-size lists to yours. As you grow your list, you can seek out people with bigger lists. If you're just starting out with no list, you can offer to have them promote you now and promote your joint venture partner's products later on when you have a bigger list.

Create a list of people you know who might partner with you. It is easier to convince someone you already have a relationship with to do a joint venture with you. If they don't think they are a good fit, they may be able to refer you to someone who is.

You want to find partners who have a similar target market to yours, but who have a different niche, that is, they are marketing a relevant but different product.

Tip: Create a letter of introduction that you can send to potential partners. It should include:
- Who you are and what you do
- Name of your product/service
- A brief description of product/service
- What is different or unique about your product or service
- The price and commission structure
- Who your ideal client is
- What support you are looking for

When seeking joint venture partners for promoting your products and services, you need to decide what commission they will receive in exchange for this. Of course, the bigger the commission, the more attractive the opportunity will be for them.

You should be offering at least a 30% commission. A 50% commission is fairly standard and some business owners will not promote for less than that. If you have a very small list and you are approaching someone with a bigger list, you may want to offer 75% or more. But these percentages are for an introductory product. You would offer less for one-on-

one coaching programs where more of your time is involved.

Decide what you feel comfortable offering, be generous, keeping in mind that you are asking people to take a risk, and that they are finding business for you.

Request a phone conversation to further discuss possibilities for mutually beneficial options. You'll also want to find out how you can support them. And remember that you are building a relationship that could last the lifetime of your business.

JV Support
In order to support JV partners you will need to create some marketing materials for them to promote you.

These include:
- 1-3 solo (exclusive) emails
- Tweets
- Facebook and LinkedIn posts
- Blog posts/articles
- Videos (optional)

Summary
Step 3: Find out where your leads are
There are many places to find high-quality leads that you can turn into clients. You need to start somewhere, so just pick one of these venues, either offline and online, and try it out. That's the only way to know if your target market is there.

Chapter 5
How Can I Build My List?

First of all, why would you want to build a list? You want to build a list so you have an audience---people to build a relationship with so they understand how you can help them and want what you have to offer. The easiest way to get them on your list is to have a gift. This is a way to give them a free taste of your service, so you can attract your ideal clients.

When I started my coaching business, I really didn't have a plan for marketing it. But the leader of my coach training program assured us that she would need more coaches to teach her methods when we graduated, and I was just planning to be one of her coaches.

Sounded so easy. No marketing, no branding, no worrying about competition---just service the clients she sends me. But the reality was that when I graduated and asked to be one of the coaches for her program, she said, "Oh, well, actually I'm not hiring any coaches right now."

That was quite a blow. I had really counted on not having to market my coaching, but now I had to if I wanted a business. It was both upsetting and discouraging. Again, I had relied on someone else to do it for me, and it fell though.

But this time around I knew a bit more about marketing. You see, back when I had ordered all those card sets and didn't know how to sell them, I had hired a marketer. He taught me his method for selling products online. His strategy was for me to create a home study course to go along with the cards, which in his opinion, would make the cards more sellable.

I spent a year creating a home study course that taught people how to use the Law of Attraction principles in Wattles' book to create a better lifestyle. It involved changing unhelpful money beliefs, visualizing what you want, and using the Law of Attraction to create wealth. It was really a coaching program for personal transformation. The course taught the same principles that I used to get myself out of debt, create a better lifestyle, and manifest an unexpected inheritance. I wanted to share those tenets with others so they could prosper also.

From that marketing experience I learned how to build a list (over 5,000), how to do a product launch with JV partners, and how to build an online presence with a website. It took a lot of work, and in the end wasn't very profitable. But in the process I became a "marketer." Since then, I have taken numerous marketing classes. So now I can share with you what I learned about how to build a list. It all hinges on your marketing strategy for converting those quality leads into subscribers.

There are only two ways to do this---**writing or speaking**. You can create a strategy by starting with one of these and still cover both through repurposing the content. Let me shorten the learning curve for you by sharing the strategies I use to convert those high-quality leads into subscribers.

Speaking

Speaking live in front of groups probably has the best return on your investment (ROI), time-wise. You are leveraging your time by getting your message out to a group of people all at once. This will take a little more prep work in that you have to design a talk. But it's a great way to get clients right away, especially if you already have a topic you can speak on.

You can present a signature talk, or a specific talk for one of your product launches, or a customized talk to a particular group of people. The personal interaction is even more effective than the less personal venues online. You get to see your audience, look into their eyes, and make authentic contact with them. They can get a better sense of you, too. They are more likely to feel connected and resonate with you.

You can give a talk in many different venues. At the end of the talk, tell them about the opt-in gift they get when they join your list. Or you can direct them to a low-end product, offer a strategy session where you will offer your higher priced product, or introduce new products to your audience.

Organizations, clubs, and local groups are always looking for speakers who don't charge a fee. You can fit that bill. You can target groups who have an interest in your topic. If you are giving a talk to an established group, they will have the venue. But if you are speaking to the general public, you'll need to find your own venue, such as a public library, a local bookstore, gift shop, friend's business place, or church.

It's best to keep your talk under an hour in duration, and 45 minutes is optimal, since you may want to have a question and answer period afterwards. Of course, if you're speaking live, your venue may have a set amount of time for your talk, so you'll have to adjust the length accordingly.

Groups

Speaking venues are similar to those for networking opportunities. Find a group to speak to that has your target in it. Make a list of groups and organizations in your locale that feature speakers. They are almost always in the market for a new speaker. Try some of these:
- Local live events
- BNI groups
- Meet-up groups
- ICF chapters
- Your local Chamber of Commerce
- Your local library
- Local business showcases
- Entrepreneur clubs
- Rotary clubs
- Toastmasters
- Support groups or clubs that have your ideal clients
- Hospitals, nursing homes, spas

You can give out your business cards, a handout, brochure, postcards, or have a group book or your own book for sale in the back of the room. Also have a sign-up sheet for your list. Don't be afraid to get into the spotlight. You have something valuable to offer, and you need to get the word out to as many people as possible.

Another angle on speaking to groups is to give a free workshop. It could be something where your attendees actually do something as they learn from you. This is a great way to get high-quality leads for your back-end coaching programs. They get first hand experience working with you and a certain percentage of those participants will want to work with you further.

Online and Offline Radio programs
Look into your local radio stations and see if they have appropriate shows you can be on. There are dozens of online radio shows that are always looking for speakers to fill their time. Google for online radio shows in your industry. Have someone who has a related product and similar niche interview you and share it with their audience.

Joint Ventures
You can do joint ventures with partners offline. Find partners who have related products and who would benefit as much as you from a cross promotion and give a talk to their audience. One of my clients created a JV partnership with a local business owner who owned a pizza parlor. My client, who was a coach in time management, gave a series of lectures on his topic at the pizza parlor, and the owner gave discount coupons each time for future pizza orders. It was a way for both of them to get new clients.

Teleseminars and Webinars
Did you know that teleseminars convert more business than any other online strategy? That's what industry leaders say, so it pays to know how to give them and profit from them. The most amazing thing about giving teleseminars is that they give you access to a worldwide audience. Teleseminars are also a better learning environment for both the student and teacher. They offer both live-interaction and a community setting that home-study courses lack.

Teleseminars are strictly audio and are delivered over the phone or online. A webinar is a teleclass with visuals, usually via a PowerPoint slide show, that's delivered online in a visual format such as Google Hangouts, Zoom, InstantTeleseminar, or GoToMeeting. Both teleclasses and webinars are great ways to speak to groups of people about your products and services worldwide, without you having to travel anywhere.

A teleseminar can be a one-time event, where people listen to you on the phone for an hour, or it can be an ongoing series. Whether used as a teaching venue for clients or as a way to promote one of your products or programs, teleseminars leverage your work hours by letting you speak to more than one person at a time.

Also, for many of us introverts, they are less intimidating than speaking in person in front of a group. They are especially good for those who are just starting out, or who can't or don't want to travel.

When used together with joint venture partners, teleseminars can be one of the fastest ways to build your list, as well as attract more clients and sell information products. You can also use a teleseminar as a preview call to promote a back-end product, such as your coaching program.

Create a signature talk that you can use as a teleseminar or webinar, and look for opportunities to deliver it. To make a signature talk, you draw from your signature program. You'll want to pick a few of your steps to cover and talk about why they are important and what results can be expected from going through them. Or you can discuss each step in some detail.

Either way, you give your audience just enough content to see the value and want more, i.e., your program. That is, give them what they need to know to lead them to what you have to offer.

Using PowerPoint as visuals for webinars
According to industry leaders, 80% of us learn more via visuals. That's why it makes sense to do a webinar, where

you have visuals to show along with the audio. You can make a PowerPoint slide show to go along with your material, and this will significantly help your audience remember what you said.

When creating a PowerPoint slide show, don't just have slides of printed bullet points that you read. Keep their interest---find photos that are eye-catching, amusing, relevant, or unusual to compliment your material. Use the PowerPoint tools to design the slide so that it has impact. Your audience will remember what you said because they'll remember the picture, especially if it's humorous.

You can add pictures, graphics and music to your webinar. But it's important to check the royalties and licenses involved. You can purchase the right to use royalty free pictures and music. Royalty-free means that you don't have to pay each time you use the image or sound clip, but you still may have to purchase the image. There are many sites where you can buy images and sound clips. But there are also plenty of royalty-free images and sound clip sites where you don't have to pay for them.

Where to get free images
www.pixabay.com
www.freeimages.com
www.morguefile.com
www.pexels.com

Writing

Below are four writing strategies you can use to generate traffic that will be quality leads for your business.

Blogging

A blog is a place where you can write about yourself, and your business. It's a place where you can share interesting tidbits about your life as well as valuable information about topics related to your products and services. This is a great place to build relationships online, because you are "talking" directly to your visitors in casual language. They can get a better feel for who you are and what you do by what you write about and how you present your material.

A blog lets you build a relationship with readers in a way that a static website can't. Readers can interact on a blog by leaving comments. When you reply to people who comment on your blog, you are creating a dialogue, the beginning of a relationship.

The main reason people blog is to get attention and gain visibility, which in turn can get them new clients. By sharing tips, suggestions, and information with your audience, you will begin to get recognized as an authority in your field. With an opt-in box on your blog page you can entice visitors to join your email list.

What can you blog about?
With a business blog, you will want to blog about subjects related to your business that will be interesting and useful to your readers and potential clients. The idea is to get them to want to return to read more blog posts, sign up for your list, and build that relationship. For a list of blog ideas go to: http://iaplifecoaches.org/resources/65-blog-ideas.pdf

Wordpress.org is a free blog software program that you can upload to your own site and it allows you to have your own domain name. WordPress provides files that you download from their site and upload to your site. Some hosting services provide a way to create a blog without downloading files, so you'll need to check on that with your hosting server.

There are developers all over the world who create plug-ins (tools) and themes for WordPress, so there are many options to choose from. Most of the plug-ins and themes are free. The easiest way to set this up is to find a WordPress site technician or web designer that can do all of this for you. Or if you are even somewhat technically inclined, you can set up a WordPress site yourself.

With various plug-ins you can connect your blog to your accounts to post automatically at Twitter, Facebook, and LinkedIn. You can also register your blog in blog directories. To find current ones, just Google "blog directories," or "blog directories – (your niche)."

Commenting on other blogs
Commenting on other people's blogs gives you added visibility because you are seen by a wider audience that is different from your own. If you leave a comment that has value and interest, you can generate interest in what you are doing. This can also lead to being invited by the blog host to present a guest blog post on their blog. Then their audience gets exposed to you and it's another way to build your list.

Search for blogs that are in your industry and make comments on their posts that relate to your posts. When you are asked to enter your URL, use the URL of one of your specific blog posts. That way you are sending traffic to your site about a relevant topic instead of just your home page. When enough people go to your blog post, it will start appearing in keyword searches more often. And of course, the more people who visit your site, the better its ranking in the search engines.

One way to get the attention of industry leaders is to comment on their blogs. Since industry leaders have lots of followers, this is a strategy that people have used to get exposure to a wider audience. It can also lead into possible joint ventures.

Guest blogging

Commenting on other blogs is a good preparation for guest blogging. You can invite people to guest blog on your blog, or you can be a guest on someone else's blog. It's actually another form of a joint venture because you are getting permission to get your material in front of someone else's audience.

---On your blog

The best way to start out is to offer guest blog spots to colleagues on your own blog. You can do exchanges with bloggers you know. Then once you have regular visitors you can offer guest post spots to higher profile people in your industry. Promoting others is a way to give first, and there's a good chance they will reciprocate.

---On other people's blogs

Guest blogging is a great way to get visibility in your field. Other people's blogs have audiences who have never heard your message, so you get to give it to a whole new group of people. Guest blogging is also a win/win situation, because you are giving the blog owner fresh content, and you are expanding your audience exponentially. Look for blogs that will put you in front of audiences that are potentially eager to hear your message.

The best way to find relevant blogs is to start with those you follow, comment on, and have a relationship with. You can also do a search for "Blog: (your niche)" or "guest post."

Tip: It's helpful to keep track of blog sites you want to be a guest on, and you can create a spreadsheet for that. Record the blog name, URL, owner and contact info, and other data about the site. When selecting blogs to write for, don't discount sites because they are too small, too new, or too unknown. They can grow and, as they do, you can become a known authority on these blogs.

Once you have your list of potential blogs, the next step is to start commenting on those blogs. You want to give valuable content, show your expertise, and help the blog owner and readers get familiar with you. Only after establishing yourself as a commenter on that blog for a while, should you approach the blog owner about a guest post.

When selecting blogs to be a guest for, study the site to discover what kind of audience they have. Ask yourself these questions:
1) Who are their major readers?
2) What level is their audience at---beginner, intermediate or advanced?
3) Are they people just looking for information, or are they people who are ready to invest in themselves and/or a coaching service?
4) What is the style of the blog posts?
5) Do they use graphics, photos, etc.?

You can contact blog owners until you find one that accepts your offer. Do this by introducing yourself. Mention your credentials, articles you've published, and your experience. Outline the idea of your article and tell them why their readers would enjoy it. When approaching a blog owner about guest blogging, be sure to explain what's in it for them, and why their readers would benefit from it. Offer exclusive content (particular post) unique to their blog.

From time to time I receive requests for a guest post on the IAPLC blog, and it's often on a topic that is not relevant to my readers. These people obviously didn't do their homework and are wasting their time and mine. So, do your homework and make sure your proposal is relevant to the blog in question.

The greatest benefits of guest blogging are that you build relationships with leaders in your field, potential joint venture partners, and a whole new group of potential clients.

Article Writing

Writing articles is another effective way to build your list. Most article directories like to see articles of about 500-700 words. And they give more exposure to articles of that size. Your articles are designed to give valuable content, information, and resources that will build trust with your prospects and filter out the people who don't resonate with you.

In your articles you will want to include the keywords (which you found from your market research) that your target market is using. Writing keyword-focused articles will help you get your webpages ranked well in search engines like Google, Yahoo and others, and thus will generate highly targeted traffic from the article directories.

Here's how it works. You submit your article to an article directory that relates to your products or services. The articles that you submit include an author's resource box where you provide information about yourself and your business, including a link to your website. Then the directory allows other publishers and webmasters to reprint your articles as long as the resource box that you carefully crafted is left intact.

Article resource box

Your resource box should emphasize the benefit of joining your list along with a description of your opt-in gift. Article directories recommend that you use both a direct link and an anchor text link in your resource box whenever possible. A direct link is one that is the URL such as, http://iaplifecoaches.org (you can see the actual URL). An anchor link is one that uses a phrase (which is all the reader sees) that has the URL embedded such as "life coach directory" which links to http://iaplifecoaches.org.

The more articles you have in the directories, the better chance you have of building your list quickly and having your targeted leads find you.

Here are some general directories you can send articles to:
www.EzineArticles.com
www.ArticlesBase.com
www.ArticleDashboard.com
www.Self-Growth.com

If you don't want to write articles or don't feel that it's the best use of your time, you can use other people's articles. Type the words 'free articles' into a search engine and you'll get page after page of websites packed with articles you can use for free. This is one way to get started so that you have content to share with your list. Just make sure the articles are relevant to your offerings.

Or you can buy professionally written articles to customize and use as your own. Once purchased, you have full rights to edit and modify the articles however you like.

Here are two sources for them:
www.ready2goarticles.com
www.6figurenewsletters.com

Email Series

The goal of a marketing strategy is to get your lead to opt-in to your list and then market to the list by building relationships and educating them about you and your work. Once you have gotten your quality lead to opt-in to your list, you will need to create a follow-up system that nurtures that lead until they are ready to buy your product(s). This system is automated through your autoresponder.

You write a series of emails (or provide links to a video series), which educates your lead about what your solution is, how you work, and anything else they need to know in order to make a buying decision. You also want to continue to give them value through free tools, resources, and information that will be useful to them.

We all have heard that you need to "touch" a prospect at least seven times before they are likely to respond to your marketing efforts, and some say many more than that. So you should have at least 7 emails in your series, and preferably more. The email series for members of my association get a weekly tip for one year---that's over 52 emails in the series.

These need to be written out, but as I said above, you can include a link to a video, so it's not such a big writing project. Your email system is designed to move the prospect through your sales funnel, so as they buy products, you will need other email series for each step of your product-buying process.

Opt-in Gift

In order to build your list, you have to move leads from the offline or online venue where you found them and onto your list in an environment that you control.

Once you find the leads, how do you get them to join your list? You need an opt-in gift. Your gift will be unique to you so that you stand out from the crowd, and your target will give you their email address in exchange for it. They are also saying yes to receiving more from you, including your marketing messages, via email.

You start this process by sending the leads to an opt-in page on your website. The wording you put on that page needs to be a compelling message that will attract people to your gift. And that message should speak specifically to your target about the problem you solve (your niche). You only want subscribers who want to learn more from you, and will love hearing from you. Then it becomes your job to nurture that relationship.

Summary
Step 4: Use a marketing strategy to build your list.
You can do that with an opt-in gift combined with a marketing strategy to encourage the right leads to subscribe to your list. Start with what you do best---either speaking or writing---and then repurpose that one into the other form if you like.

Chapter 6
How Can I Use Social Media to Get Clients?

Once you have a marketing strategy that uses either writing and/or speaking, then you can find an offline or online platform. We have talked about offline platforms such as meetings, and events. The best and most popular platform to use online is social media. And one of the most often asked questions is how to USE social media to find clients?

When I first started out trying hard to get clients, I felt like the key to the entrepreneurial world was still eluding me. I wondered if I would really be able to get this one off the ground. I was doing all the things the industry gurus said to do---article writing, blogging, YouTube videos, Facebook posts, Twitter tweets, Pinterest pins, and LinkedIn discussions. And it was driving me crazy. I could barely keep up with it all. But I kept going.

What happened next really surprised me! As I was going over my statistics, I discovered that 80% of my website traffic was coming from one source--the LinkedIn coaches group that I had started a few years earlier. It seemed logical that I should focus my marketing to my own group on LinkedIn.

That turned out to be a good idea because now 6 years later, that group which has grown to over 15,000 members, is where almost all of my business comes from. And they all fit my target market criteria, they all know who I am because they hear from me on a regular basis. Now I just market to my group and save myself a lot of time and money.

So, creating your own group online is one of the best places to find high-quality leads where you can develop the "know, like, and trust" factor. But I'm going to share several other sources you can use while you're building your group.

Marketing on social media is one of the fastest and easiest ways to get clients, if you know how to use the different networks effectively. You can use Social Media for the following:
- Getting leads
- Finding people who are ready for your solution
- Making connections with potential buyers
- Making connections with potential joint venture partners

Important: Keep these business tasks in mind when using social media--otherwise you will go down the proverbial rabbit hole. Here are some tips for using social media as a platform for your marketing strategies.

How to not waste time on social media

There are several different ways that you can avoid wasting time on social media and stay focused on the above business tasks. First of all, you want to plan out a strategy and then you want to follow it! That means that you need to have a formal, written-out plan (yes—in writing—and right in front of you) of what you will be doing whenever you're on social media.

For example let's say you're going to use LinkedIn for your social media groups. You will allot time for commenting on discussions, posting discussions, and inviting people to connect with you. You will not be reading all the entries in your feed, clicking on other people's blog posts and reading them, and other distracting things---unless you are doing research.

A second strategy for not wasting time on social media is to give yourself a time limit when you're on there. For the above example, you could allot yourself 5 minutes for commenting on other people's discussions, 5 minutes for posting your own discussion, and 5 minutes for sending out 3-5 connection requests. That would be 15 minutes a day that you allowed yourself for going on LinkedIn.

The third strategy to implement is to just start with one social media site and work with it until you start getting consistent results. Only then should you think about adding, one at a time, more social media sites, to increase your workload.

Know which social media to use

In order to know which social media site you should be working with, you need to revisit your foundation work in the first chapters of this book. That means you have clearly defined your target market, know where they hang out, and what their interests are. And you know the solutions you can bring to the problems they are having.

In selecting a social media site, consider the culture of that network. For example, is it mostly a business culture or is it more a social culture?

We can see that LinkedIn is much more business-oriented in its culture then Facebook, Twitter, or YouTube. Facebook is more social and is more geared to people who are connecting with friends and family. So if your target market is moms, Facebook may be the best place for you to be doing your marketing. But if your target market is executives, then LinkedIn would be the better place to do your marketing.

Another aspect to consider: is your business a B2B or B2C? (That means business-to-business or business-to-customer.) If you are a B2B, then you would probably be more likely to find your target market on LinkedIn where it's a more business-like atmosphere. If you are a B2C, you may want to focus on Facebook, YouTube, or Twitter.

As I said, I found that the best network for me was LinkedIn. Having just this one marketing focus freed up a large amount of my time. I was able to develop more products and to spend more time engaging with people online. I had more time for coaching too, and began taking on more private clients. My businesses started growing and I was happier.

So that's why I recommend that you pick one platform and focus on it. Mastering one marketing strategy will put you farther ahead, faster, than trying to keep up with many strategies on the different social media networks.

Grow your reach on social media

It's quality, not quantity that matters when you're building a list, growing your audience, or looking for clients. It's better to have a small, responsive group of people that are more likely to become buyers, then a large group of unresponsive people who are mainly freebie seekers.

You can expand your reach in social media best by partnering with influencers. Influencers are people who have large or medium size lists or audiences that are responsive to their offers and contain your target market. You can find influencers in your industry by Googling your topic and seeing which websites come up on the first pages. Those are most likely to be the big influencers. You can also look on Amazon in your topic under books and see what the most popular books are on your topic, because those authors may also be influencers.

Another way to expand your reach is to be proactive and that means commenting on discussions in the groups that you belong to, asking questions, and engaging people in conversations. And of course that all should lead to setting up private conversations with qualified leads.

With both Facebook and LinkedIn, your goal should be to grow your own group.

Build your list with social media
Be connection-selective

In order to build your list with social media you want to keep in mind that you are looking for **quality** leads not just quantity. So be "connections selective." That means when you're connecting with people, be selective about who you're connecting with. Try to only connect with people who you think are qualified leads or qualified joint venture partners. Then once you connect with people take the time to build rapport. It's something you would do with anyone you meet---establish a relationship.

Don't try to sell too soon
You also want to resist the urge to make an offer too soon after you've made a connection. This is a trap that many marketers fall into and you should avoid at all costs. That's the one thing that can turn off a new subscriber or prospective client. Take the time to nurture that new connection. You want to show them that you're there to help them. Nurture them with information, valuable content, and resources. In order to do that you probably won't be able to come up with enough content yourself. So what most marketers do is become content curators.

Become a content curator
Content curation involves finding other people's good stuff, summarizing it, and sharing it. By sharing other people's content, you are making a win/win/win situation for everyone involved. It will not only build relationships with your audience, but also with those whose content you share. How will they know that you've shared their content? One way is to tag them in a comment in the discussion area.

Nurturing system
You also want to have a system for nurturing those leads and that should include a content-sharing campaign for the groups that you are in on Facebook or LinkedIn or groups that you own. You also want to have a system for nurturing your leads once they get on your list. That means a series of emails that educate them further on helping them with the problem that you solve.

Follow-up system
You also need a system for follow-up. So for follow-up, I'm referring to calling back people that you have spoken to see how they're doing, ask them if they need any more

information or help, and make sure that they are getting the emails that you have set up on your autoresponder.

Where to find content to share

I've mentioned several times now that you need to be sharing valuable content with your audience. So you might ask where do you get this content? I have a couple sources for you. The sites below collect content and show what's trending. By visiting these sites you can see what people are talking about and what is popular and get links for content you can share.
- Buzzumo.com
- Scoop.it
- Feedly.com

You can also look for sites that are related to your topic or products and your competitors' sites where you can share some of their content.

I have a list of other people's sites that have blogs with great information, which I think would be of value to my audience. Part of my content sharing campaign includes links to those people's best blog posts. This is something that you can incorporate into your follow-up system for sharing content.

Keep track of your postings

The way to keep track of your postings is to create an editorial calendar and you can do this on an Excel spreadsheet. You can list the dates that you are going to post content and then list the title that you want to use and details about it, and a link if you're linking to something.

You can also use this calendar to plan ahead for any events launches or other important dates of things that you want to share with your audience, as well as posts for promoting your joint venture partners.

Summary
Step 5: Use social media to get your leads
Now you can choose one social media site to focus on and master marketing using your chosen marketing strategy on that network.

Chapter 7
How Do I Convert Leads Into Clients?

Now that you have attracted quality leads to join your list, nurtured them, and gotten them interested in your work, the next step to have a sales conversation with your potential client. Most coaches offer a complimentary enrollment conversation in which they discover whether the client's needs fit with the coach's program. These conversations can be called sales calls, free consultations, strategy sessions, discovery sessions, enrollment conversations, or pre-screening conversations.

Whatever you call it, in this phone conversation you will be on a fact-finding mission to gather as much information as you can about that person's situation and background to see if they are a good fit. You will also want to gain some insight into the prospects' financial ability to hire you as a coach, as well as how motivated they are to do so.

Note: That means that this conversation is NOT a free coaching session where you give them a taste of your style of coaching. Free coaching sessions usually end up with the potential client thinking that they have enough for now and don't sign up as a client.

Tips for getting sales calls
Getting people to sign-up for a free consultation is a sale in itself. So treat it like a product itself and position it in an attractive way. One way to do that is to give it an eye-catching name, such as "Business Breakthrough Session," "Find Your Ideal Weight Now Coaching Session" or "Quick Marketing Strategy Session."

So if you are treating this like a product, you need a way to offer it. That could be a link to a sign-up page on your website, or an invitation in your email series (preferably both).

You can list 3 to 5 bullet points as to what they will get out of the session. They want to know what they can walk away with. Make the benefits of your session specific and tangible. If you give them some compelling expectations, they will be more likely to choose YOUR conversation invitation over someone else's.

The Sales Conversation
The sales or enrollment conversation is part of your marketing strategy. No matter how good you are as a coach, consultant, or other service-based business owner, you must master the sales process. But it doesn't have to be difficult. Most of us shy away from sales because of the stigma it conjures up---the aggressive salesman who makes you feel pressured to purchase something. So now when we are in the sales person position, we overcompensate for not

wanting to sound like the aggressive sales person, and go to the other extreme of being too lax in our selling skills.

But sales skills in the enrollment conversations are the key to a coach's success in business. If you can't enroll clients into your programs, you don't have a business. But most coaches didn't get "sales" training in coach training. You learned how to be a coach, but not necessarily how to be a salesperson.

You need some kind of sales training. There are so many different kinds of sales training out there. When I participated in a fancy year-long group coaching program with a 7-figure coach, we were taught 23 steps to take during an enrollment conversation. That's a lot of steps to remember. And what I found was that it was hard to stick to the formula. Prospects can pull you in all different directions---especially if you let them do most of the talking. (And a good sales person lets the prospect do most of the talking.)

I heard a teleclass by a business coach who said that even 6-7 figure coaches only get 25-30% conversions in their conversations and that's what you should shoot for. That means if you want 5 new clients a month, you need to have 20 conversations a month. Think about that for a minute---that is 20 hours a month, plus the time it takes to find those 20 people.

But actually, there's an easier way. You could focus on improving your conversion rate instead. What if that 25-30% was increased to 50-75%? Then you would only need 7-10 conversations per month to get those 5 clients.

Here are some tips about how you can improve that conversion rate.
    1. Check inside yourself to see what beliefs are preventing you from getting sales – sometimes

some personal development is necessary to increase sales
2. Get crystal clear on who your ideal target market is so you are targeting the right people who are the best fit for your programs
3. Take the time to establish rapport with your prospect---it's probably the most important part of the sales conversation
4. Establish the agenda for the conversation so they know what to expect and understand that you are in charge of the content of the conversation
5. Learn how to establish the gap between where they are at and where they want to go, and how your solution can bridge that gap
6. Know how to articulate the value of your program or service
7. Speak from the heart, offer your solution, and support them in deciding the right path for them---be their advocate for change
8. Learn how to confidently ask for the sale, without feeling salesy
9. Transform objections into opportunities for you to serve them - address these objections for the prospect, so they can make their decision with confidence. Here's your opportunity to actually coach them to take action based on a better understanding of the value you offer, instead of a fear-based decision.
10. Nurture a relationship with your prospects way before the conversation. Give them plenty of free content, information and resources so that by the time they get around to making an appointment with you, they are already practically sold on you and your service.

Your business depends on the outcome of these enrollment conversations, so I want you to understand how important they are. You should set a goal for how many conversations you want to have every month, based on the number of clients you want per month, and set up your marketing to secure those appointments. Limit them to 30 to 60 minutes and be firm about this. Then track your conversion rate for them. I think an acceptable rate is more like 50%. That means half of your conversations should turn into enrolled clients. But shoot for 80-90%.

If you're just starting out, it's a good idea to hook-up with a colleague and practice your conversation. You want to be perfectly comfortable exploring someone else's personal situation, uncovering their pain points, helping them create a vision of a better future, wrapping your program key points around their needs, and finally asking for the money. Once you feel comfortable with these conversations, your confidence will increase, and your conversions will improve.

Follow-up
Where many coaches leave money on the table is in not following up with prospects who didn't enroll. They may have other issues that they didn't bring up. They may have to rearrange their finances and are too embarrassed to tell you. Or they may need to make sure they can fit your program into their schedule. Whatever the reason, stay in touch with them until they are ready to enroll, or give you a definite no.

The enrollment conversation is the KEY area for attracting clients. If you know how to explore the potential client's needs and articulate the value you offer, you will get clients.

Metrics – tracking your sales
The essential element in implementing any marketing strategy is to know where you stand by knowing your numbers before you start. This is what we call your metrics. Then, as you implement sales-boosting strategies, you need

to measure how each one does. If you're not testing and measuring everything you do, you won't know what works and what doesn't work.

By tracking your results, you can refine, change, or cancel actions before they cost you too much time and/or money. And that means not only what you spend directly, but also what money you are leaving on the table by not doing something that could make a better profit.

When you see that something didn't work very well, try another strategy. Keep doing that until you find something that works. You may have to try various marketing ideas before you get the results you are after.

Using a conversion analysis system will help you track your conversion rates at every point of your sales path and discover where the weak spots are. How do you do that?

The sales path looks like this:
A. Visitors → B. Opt-ins → C. Sales conversation →
D. Product sales - Clients

| A. Visitors | B. Opt-ins | C. Sales conversation | D. Product Sale/Clients |

Point A
Start your analysis with how many visitors you have to your site per day. If you're not getting a certain amount every day, you need to see where you can improve your marketing to drive visitors to your site.

Point B
Next you need to know what percentage of those visitors opt-in to your list. Your offer has to be irresistible in order to compete with all the other free offers on the Internet in your field.

Point C
Then how many enrollment appointments are you getting from your list? Are people asking for them every week? Check your statistics of how many subscribers you are getting per week and then how many appointments are being made and determine the conversion rate.

Point D
The final stage of your sales path is from the number of people who have an enrollment conversation to the number of them that purchase a product or service from you. If it's not a good rate, then you will need to do something at that point to increase the conversion rate.

When in doubt about how to improve your conversions, find a colleague, client, coach, or mentor to help you troubleshoot the problem. Many times it's easier for others to see where the weakness is, than yourself. Be sure to take a look at all four points in your sales path.

Having a system will make tracking easier. Start a spreadsheet with the above four A-D points on it and keep track of your conversion rates. This way you will not only have the big picture of your progress, but also have genuine statistics you can use when inviting people to joint venture with you.

Summary

Step 6: Learn how to sell by improving your conversion rate and tracking your sales

If you are going to have a business, you need to know how to sell. As a coach or consultant, your mindset should be that sales is just about having a conversation with someone who has already expressed interest in your product and helping them make the decision to move forward.

Chapter 8
How Can I Retain Clients?

After you've gone to all the effort of getting a client, how do you make sure that they stick with you at least through your program, but potentially for many years to come? Of course you want a well-designed product or service that can hold your client's interest and give high value so they will want to stay I the program.

The best way to retain clients and sell more products to them, is to nurture them and have a follow-up system in place for doing that.

Keep your follow-up system simple so it doesn't overwhelm you. You can create an email series that includes links to interesting articles, resources, tools, videos, and other helpful information. That way you set it up once and it's in place for all your clients. You can also survey your clients to find out what they need next and then create next step products for them.

Nurture your clients

Once you get clients, you want to help them feel like you really care about them and are there for them. Here are several ways that you can nurture your clients.

1- Hangout where they hangout

If you know that they are in groups on LinkedIn or Facebook, hang out with those groups, comment on people's discussions, look for your clients comments in those groups and comment on them. You can also go to their own LinkedIn profile page and send them a message, and/or endorse them.

You can also hang out where they hang out offline. That could be places like community groups, book clubs, or any events that are happening in your locality.

2- Read the same publications

Another way is to read publications that they read. One way to find out what they read is to ask them for recommendations on what they are reading. This can be books, journals, magazines even blogs. Find out what they're reading and read the same things. This can also include neighborhood publications, church bulletins and other club publications that both may be members of.

3- Send them a link

A third way that you can keep in touch and nurture your clients is to send them a link to an article that you think would be valuable for them to read. It can be either one of your own or one of somebody else's. This is a great way to share content with them and let them know that you are thinking of them. It makes them feel special.

4- Interview them

Another way to nurture your clients is to ask to interview your client. Everyone likes to be thought of as the expert, so if you have a podcast or radio show or even just want to promote that client to your list, you can do an interview with them. You can make either an audio or video and this will add to your credibility because you're speaking with an expert. But it'll also be promoting your client and it's just a great way to stay in touch with them and give them a boost.

5- Ask for a comment

Another way to keep in touch with your client is to ask them to comment on one of your articles. Say you post an article in Ezine article directory or LinkedIn's Pulse, or any other publication online and just ask them to read the article and comment on it. Of course it should be an article that they would find interesting. It could also be a brochure or a sales page or any other kind of online publication that you would like their comments and feedback on. It's just another way to make a touch with them and let them know that you're thinking about them.

6- Send hand-written notes

Send a handwritten note is one of the best ways to appreciate your client. And you can do that for just about any conceivable reason. Of course you always want to send them a thank you note if they've done something for you such as giving you feedback or commenting on one of your articles. You're just going to be remembered more by taking the time to send a personal note to them in the mail. And that's because hardly anyone ever does that anymore. So you're going to stand out for doing something extra for them.

7- Have a Client Appreciation Night.
A wonderful way to support your clients is to have a client appreciation night. That's where you could have the clients come to your home if you're doing it locally, and just have a little get-together with them. If you're doing it online you could have a virtual appreciation night. This could be an evening where you can have some extra training or a little extra group coaching for them---just a little something extra to show your appreciation for them. You can do this monthly, quarterly, bi-annually, or annually. It's just something that you can do to show them you appreciate them and something that is on a bigger scale than your normal interactions with them.

8- Send them a gift
Last but not least is a way to keep in touch with your client and nurture them by sending them a gift. It can be anything like a plaque or stone with the word "success" on it, all the way up to a gift certificate from their favorite store or somewhere like Amazon where you know they shop. Most people can use that kind of gift certificate. Scale your gift's value according to the value of the program your client is paying you for. Sending a gift is just another way that you can appreciate your clients and let them know that you're thinking of them.

9- Give them a phone call
One of my coaches used to call me up unexpectedly just to see how I was doing that day. Sometimes it came on days when I really needed a boost and her call changed the course of the day for me. Everyone likes unexpected surprises and a phone call always shows that you care about them.

10- Add them to an email series
Be sure to set up your system so that when someone buys your product/service, they are added to a list for that product. You can have this automated. Then you can create

an email series that give them tips about using the product or service, benefits they can be reminded of, and other tips that would be helpful to them.

Provide Value

A saying in the coaching industry is that the money is in the follow-up. And it's so true. That's because it's much easier and more cost effective to sell a current or former client a new product than it is to find a new client. Most of your marketing efforts and costs will go towards getting new clients. But once you have them, you are leaving even more money on the table by not nurturing them with follow-up and creating more products for them to consume.

It took me a while to figure this out. I was great at coming up with products to sell, but they weren't very congruent with each other. By that I mean, they didn't follow in a strategically thought-out sales funnel. If you create more products than your coaching program, make sure they are congruent with your overall niche or specialty.

What is a sales funnel? It's the progression of your products that you offer from the least expensive to the most expensive. Here's an illustration:

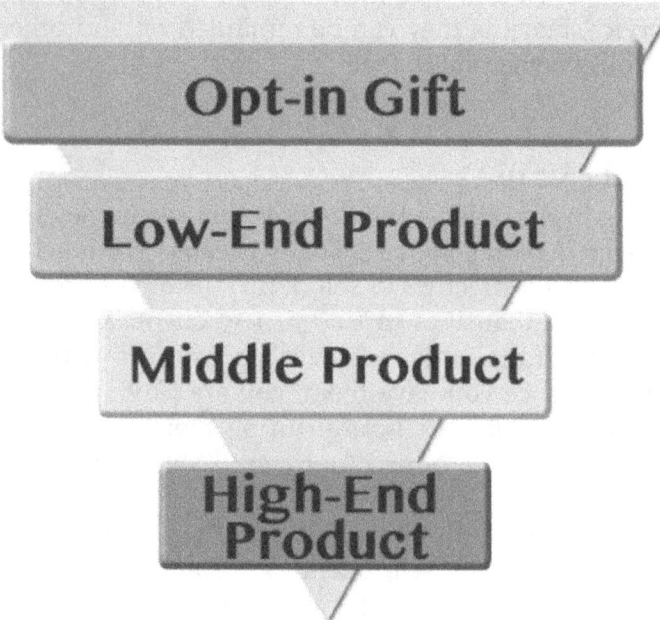

The sales funnel starts with your opt-in gift or freebie. This is your lead-generation magnet and it should be something to entice your potential client to find out more about how you can help them by opting into your list. If you have a high-quality gift, you will attract high-quality leads, so it's important to put some thought into this.

The next step in your funnel may be a low-cost item, one that gives a prospect a taste of your work by giving a partial solution to a problem related to the bigger problem. This can be in the price range of $7 to $197. Then once they consume that, they may want further help. That's when you can offer a middle level product like a home study course or a group coaching program to address the same problem in greater detail. Then your high-end offer would be your one-on-one coaching program at the highest investment level.

When you're starting out, you may help a client solve a particular problem. But once your client gets the solution, there will be other problems that come up, some of which you can also solve. That's where you can introduce another service that will help them with that new problem. It's a much easier sell because they already know, like, and trust you.

Summary
Step 7: Nurture your clients and provide continuing value
Once you get a client, you will want to build and further the relationship with them by nurturing them and providing more and more value. That way you will have clients that stay with you much longer, and you will have less marketing to do.

Chapter 9
What's the Next Step?

Now you have the 7 essential steps you need to get more clients. Let's review them.

Step 1: Carefully define your target and niche
Step 2: Do your market research in order to create a brand and drive appropriate traffic to your site
Step 3: Find out where your leads are
Step 4: Create a marketing strategy to build your list
Step 5: Use social media to get your leads
Step 6: Learn how to sell, improve your conversion rate, and track your sales
Step 7: Nurture your clients and provide continuing value

Now, this is just the beginning. Whether you have been struggling to get clients, dealing with social media overwhelm, or are just tired of working so hard with few results...

Imagine what it would be like if you had access to regular business and marketing training. And you were endorsed by an international organization that promoted your coaching business. How great would that feel? It would feel pretty amazing, right?

The Next Step
If you are a coach who would like to get high quality business and marketing training, credibility, and more visibility, become a member of the International Association of Professional Life Coaches® (IAPLC).

The association combines a premier user-friendly international online directory with group business-building activities for its members so they can grow their coaching businesses and get more clients. Members must meet certain criteria based on training, coaching experience and client references, to be listed.

If you want more marketing training, check out our Life Coach Business Academy, which offers courses on marketing specifically designed for coaches.

To become a member, enroll in the academy, take a class, or download any of our coaching business resources, visit:
www.iaplifecoaches.org

Praise for
"The 7 Essential Steps to Get More Clients"

"Jeannette's book, like all her others, is filled with simple, essential, practical tools to help coaches transform their passion for empowering others into profitable professions that fulfill them and their clients physically, mentally, emotionally and spiritually--one baby step at a time. Bravo, Jeannette!" ~ Deborah Jane Wells, Board-Certified Empowerment Coach, www.djwlifecoach.com

"Jeannette Koczela's facility and knowledge within the field of coaching is clearly evident in her newest book. She turns her practiced eye to the subjects of greatest concern to coaches: how to help as many people as possible and how to have a financially lucrative business.

"The book is replete with valuable insights, resources and practical knowledge. The format she uses is one which resonates well with coaching; namely, the asking and answering of questions, She presents her informative content as the answers to important questions coaches will have while working to build their businesses. The reader feels as though they have a caring, knowledgeable mentor or coach taking them by the hand and leading them through the challenges and difficulties of designing his or her own business.

"This is a must-read for coaches who want to build financially lucrative businesses, helping many individuals on their journeys of transformation." ~ Dr. Simone Ravicz, www.successbraincoach.com

"I found this book to be very informative. To market any business you need a system. This book is an easy read and would be beneficial to any entrepreneur starting a business and not knowing what to do first." ~ **Davida Shensky, founder** - Career Performance Institute

"Jeannette covers everything I ever wanted to know about getting more clients. I loved the detail she goes into so I can follow her examples easily." ~ **Boni Oian,** www.claimyourlifewithboni.com

"Once again Jeannette Koczela shares her expertise, insight, knowledge, and wisdom with us in her new book. The book is full of tips, tricks, and tools to help the aspiring coach or consultant launch, maintain and move forward with their business. Filled with lots of "how to" nuggets and gems like using spreadsheet to track your marketing is priceless! Bravo Jeannette in writing a profoundly comprehensive, practical book!" ~ Veronica Hislop, Em-Powered-Solutions-Life Relationship, www.empowered-solutions.ca

www.ingramcontent.com/pod-product-compliance
Lightning Source LLC
Chambersburg PA
CBHW060411190526
45169CB00002B/856